Choices

Choices

Learning to hear God's voice

Finding your way through

- the Bible
- inner peace
- events
- advice

and much more

**Martin and Elizabeth
Goldsmith**

Authentic

LONDON ● COLORADO SPRINGS ● HYDERABAD

This edition first printed 2007 by Authentic Media
9 Holdom Avenue, Bletchley, Milton Keynes, Bucks., UK
1820 Jet Stream Drive, Colorado Springs, USA
OM Authentic Media, Jeedimetla Village
Secunderabad 500 055, A.P., India
www.authenticmedia.co.uk

Authentic Media is a division of IBS-STL UK, a company limited by
guarantee (registered charity no. 270162)

British Library Cataloguing-in-Publication Data
A catalogue record for this book is available from the British Library

ISBN-13 978-1-85078-736-5
ISBN-10: 1-85078-736-0

Unless otherwise stated, Scripture quotations in this publication are
from the Holy Bible, New International Version. Copyright © 1973,
1978, 1984 International Bible Society. Published in Great Britain by
Hodder & Stoughton Ltd.

Cover design by fourninezero design.
Print Management by Adare Carwin
Printed in Great Britain by J.H. Haynes & Co., Sparkford

Contents

One

Questions of Guidance

Young people long to know what God's purpose is for their future. What professional calling should they follow? Should they go overseas for a short spell to gain wider experience? Some feel called to 'full-time' ministry either in their own country or overseas, but don't know how best to prepare for this calling.

> God's purpose ...for their future

We visit many churches and Christian Unions both in Britain and in other countries. As a result many people come to us to ask questions or share personal problems. It seems inevitable that we frequently face questions concerning guidance.

Throughout our lives all of us constantly have to make decisions which involve guidance. Is it right at this stage to change our job, or move house? Which church should we link up with locally? Should we join a rather stagnant local church or travel a few miles to a warmer Bible-teaching fellowship? As we begin to earn more, so we have more money to give away: what missions, Christian workers or other causes should we support? As the years go by we seem to have an ever-increasing list of prayer needs presented to us: should we concentrate our prayers on a few or pray generally for the many? Likewise there are more and more calls upon our time. I know this is a problem for our family. What should be the balance between family or home responsibilities and the pressing calls of Christian ministry? And, which areas of ministry should have priority? Whatever our situations all of us will constantly face decisions of different sorts in which we as Christians need to know the will of God for us.

... decisions which involve guidance

Meet Elizabeth

At the time each issue seems tremendously important and we earnestly try to hear the voice of God. And it is true that often apparently quite small decisions actually affect the whole future course of one's life. Thus Elizabeth delayed her university studies a year in order to help her parents in the old people's home which they ran. If she had not done this, she would have gone overseas as a missionary a year earlier and we should perhaps not have met each other. So that relatively minor

What should be the balance ...?

decision to help her parents actually altered the whole course of her life.

On the other hand, we often feel that God's overall guidance of our lives has been more important than the little details of specific issues. As we look back over what God has done for us, we praise him more for the broad sweeps of his paint brush than for the more detailed shading day by day. In fact, our weakness and sin has meant that we have often failed the Lord and disobeyed him in particular matters, but nevertheless, we are gratefully aware that this does not deflect God from his overall leading of our lives. It is such a reassuring and comforting truth to know that with our gracious Father even 'if we are faithless, he remains faithful'.   2 Timothy 2:13

It's not easy!

Some years ago, I was invited to a large youth conference where the other main speaker was a powerful and gifted communicator.

He was a real man of God, but I had very definite doubts about his message. Having carefully defined his use of the word 'miracle' as an act of God which was not according to the natural order, he then stressed that every Christian should experience such supernatural miracles every day. I too believe in a God who works miracles. My wife and I have frequently experienced the

> ...each issue seems tremendously important...

Lord's gracious working of miracles. But we cannot say that this is a normal daily event for us. I wondered what this speaker's emphasis would mean for the young Christians listening with open hearts to what he said. Quite a few of them were new believers and some were insecure and unstable personally.

With these deep questionings in my heart, I discussed the matter with one of the other leaders at the conference. This conversation gave me a further perspective on how miracles can be a part of God's leading. We quickly discovered that our Christian lives had followed quite different paths, but came to the same conclusion. Both of us had to learn to walk by faith and sight. He came from a somewhat Victorian Christian home which was very godly, strong in biblical teaching and morally upright. But he grew up with little experience of the more direct working of God – and miracles were almost anathema! Now, as a mature Christian leader, he was beginning to move into, what were for him, new areas of faith. He was seeing God working miracles in answer to believing prayer.

...deep questionings in my heart...

Meet Martin

My background was different. When I first became a committed Christian at university, my knowledge of Christian matters was negligible.

I was thrilled with my new faith in Christ and his saving work for me, but the tree of my faith lacked deeper roots. Was it all just psychological?

Does God really exist? Does the cross of Jesus really deal with our sins? Did Jesus really rise from the dead? My joyful exuberance in Christ could be easily uprooted and shattered. But the Lord met me more than halfway. He worked miracle upon miracle in answer to prayer. When I prayed, things happened. When I asked the Lord for guidance, the way ahead became crystal clear. It was marvellous to see the reality of God. My God was alive and at work.

> **Was it all just psychological?**

But as I have gone on in my walk with the Lord, my prayers have not always been answered at all! And as I get older, it seems to become less easy to discern the will of God in specific decisions and I need to use what is sometimes called 'sanctified common sense'. I feel that God has been saying to me, 'In your early days as a believer I allowed you to walk by sight, because you were so weak. Now you must learn to walk by faith.

Wherever you are in walking with the Lord, this book is written out of the conviction that God wants to guide you and all his people today. Our prayer is that everyone who reads the following six

> **God's love and care for each of us is personal ...**

chapters will come away with a deeper sense of assurance and calling in whatever situation they are in. We do not know our readers individually. But God does. His love and care for each of us is personal and precious. That's why Jesus is often called the 'Guide' or the 'Good Shepherd', the one who died for us, his sheep.

OVER TO YOU

You will find it very helpful to write answers to these questions, rather than merely think about them.

1. Can you trace God's overall guidance of your life?

2. Have you faced the need for direct guidance recently? If so, how did you expect God to show you his will? And did he?

3. Have you ever experienced God guiding you through your conscience? Did you obey?

Two

Our God Guides

What principles or patterns of guidance can we find in the Bible? Who does God guide and how?

As on every subject, so in the question of guidance, we need to be soundly based in Scripture which is God's word to teach and lead us. Our ideas on practical subjects need to be soundly biblical and not just based on experience.

The Scriptures reassure us that God does not simply bring us to saving faith in himself and then leave us to our own devices. No, he takes us by the hand and leads us graciously and safely through life. This does not mean that we miss the normal heartaches, problems or tragedies of life in a fallen world, but in all situations we have the assurance of God's guiding presence with us. Thus, in Psalm 32:8 God says: 'I will instruct you and teach you the way you should go; I will counsel you and watch over you.' The context of this verse is that David was going through 'a time of

> God does not ... leave us to our own devices

Psalm 32:6 distress' which is also described as a 'rush of great waters'.

The Psalms constantly affirm this foundational fact that God leads his people. Psalm 48 concludes with this triumphant declaration: 'He will be our guide even to the end.' The psalmist declares that this is the nature of our God for <div style="float:left">Psalm 48:14</div> ever and ever. He says that we are to pass on this good news from generation to generation – God is our guide! Psalm 78 adds the further <div style="float:left">Psalm 78:72</div> assurance that God guides us 'with skilful hands'. We may marvel at the skill of a pilot bringing an enormous tanker through a shallow channel into port. I remember being guided by tribal Christians to a remote village. We struggled through thick jungle and over a high range of hills for many hours. I had no idea of the way, but I had every confidence in the guidance of my friends. God's guidance is even more certain and 'skilful' than that of any person. How wonderful!

Are you in a wilderness?

...the heartaches, problems or tragedies of life ...

In Psalm 78:52 the picture used is that of a shepherd. God led his people 'like sheep', 'like a flock'. This imagery of God as our shepherd comes again and again throughout the Old Testament. The theme is taken up in the New Testament with Jesus as the perfect shepherd who knows his sheep and 'leads them'. The sheep know the voice of the shepherd, and trust him, so they 'follow him' when he 'goes on ahead of them'. Guidance is not just God speaking to us from afar and telling us what to do or where to go, but rather he himself leads the way and goes with us, both into the 'green pastures' and also in the dangers and sufferings of the wilderness. The shepherd not only guides, but also leads from the front.

John 10:3

John 10:4

Jesus himself knew this amazing experience of being led in the wilderness. In Luke 4:1–2 Jesus was led 'by the spirit . . . in the wilderness'. For Jesus there was apparently no contradiction between being in the Spirit and in the wilderness. Although he was in Satan's territory assailed by fierce temptation, he was still 'in the Spirit' and was being led. In fact, this is the only place in the Gospels where it is clearly stated that Jesus was led or guided by God. God does lead his people and did lead his Son Jesus, but the leading of God is particularly to be experienced when we are in the wilderness.

God leads his people . . .

The final book of the Bible, the book of Revelation, shows us, however, that the wilderness is not the end of the story. There is a promised land. In Revelation 7 we see into heaven itself. We meet those 'who have come out of the great tribulation' and are now before the throne of God where the wilderness sufferings are ended. The Lord 'will guide them to springs of living water', he 'will wipe away every tear from their eyes'.

Revelation 7:14

Revelation 7:17

It is good to be constantly reminded that our God does guide. He leads us even in the wilderness – in fact, particularly in the wilderness. His ultimate purpose and aim is to bring us into his glory.

Hand in hand with the Father

...people of all races and types...

In the Old Testament only Israel really experiences the guidance of God. The New Testament emphasizes that the God of Israel wants to have people of all races and types as his children. All who receive Jesus Christ and believe in his name can now become children of God. No longer does our relationship with God depend on our background. We can be born again as children of the heavenly Father, 'not of blood nor of the will of the flesh nor of the will of man, but of God'. Men and women of every race, every class, every educational background can have God as their Father.

John 1:13

Paul links the fact that we are children of God with the further truth that we are led by God's spirit. It is a sure mark that we are God's children if we are led by his Spirit. It is intimacy with God, so that we can call God 'Abba, Father' like a child with his daddy. A father has special responsibility for his children.

Romans 8:14

I sometimes watch the married students at the college where I teach. It is heartwarming to see a father happily cuddling his baby or proudly leading his little child by the hand as they walk through the woods.

In my tutorial group this year I have a young mother who often feeds her baby during our group worship times. It is beautiful to see her joy as she smiles into the face of her suckling child. We see something of God's relationship to us through the picture of human parents and their children.

God is our loving Father. He cares and provides for us. He teaches us what is right and wrong in his sight. He protects us. He leads us and takes us by the hand as we walk through life.

Again we notice in Romans 8 the dual context of our being led by the Spirit of God our Father. We do not escape the reality that we shall 'suffer with him'. But again the goal is that 'we may also be glorified with him'.

Romans 8:17

God's overall guidance

Later we shall look at how God guides us with regard to specific decisions. But at this stage we want to look a little at the overall purposes of God into which the details of daily life must fit. It is hard to find God's will in these smaller matters if we do not understand the fundamentals of God's character, the way he works and the sort of things he desires.

We have sometimes enjoyed watching people

We do not escape reality ...

playing the 'husbands and wives' game at parties or on television. 'What would your husband say if . . . ?', 'What would your wife do if . . . ?' 'Does your husband/wife like it when you . . .?' Such questions depend on a married couple living together and sharing in such a way that they know each other's minds. We have now been married for over forty years and often know what the other is thinking or feeling without any need for words. Likewise in our relationship with God it is good to walk closely with him so that we gradually learn what sort of decisions please him. We need to be steeped in the Scriptures which reveal to us the character and mind of the Lord. We are not only reading the Bible in the hope that we may get a direct 'word from the Lord' relevant to life now, but also to store up any understanding of God's ways. Then we may be able to make daily decisions in accordance with his overall will.

When children are small, parents need to give specific instructions on every detail of life. As children grow up within the family, they learn what patterns of behaviour are expected. They can then begin to think out right answers for new situations without needing to be guided in every matter by their parents. New and immature Christians may need specific words from the Lord on minor issues of behaviour, but hopefully we will mature and grow in knowledge of God's overall will for his people.

...we gradually learn what sort of decisions please him

For example, this 'mind of Christ' applies to the choice of a life partner for marriage. Of course we want definite assurance from the Lord before we decide to get engaged. But we also want to ask more general questions. We know from the Bible that we are not to be 'mismated with unbelievers'. We don't therefore, need guidance as to whether we should have a serious relationship with a non-Christian. God's will is clear. We know people who have taken a liking to a non-Christian and then have gone to the Bible in the hope that they might find a verse which may encourage them to go ahead with the relationship. Then they often twist the meaning of a verse to suit the guidance they wanted. Or they may go from Christian friend to Christian friend asking their opinion concerning this possible relationship. Eventually they will probably find someone foolish enough to say what was desired. They then reassure themselves that their decision was supported by other Christians. Actually they did not need to look for guidance at all – God's will was clear and obvious from his word. It was clearly 'No!'

1 Cor. 2:16

2 Cor. 6:14 RSV

> **It was clearly 'No!'**

What is God's overall purpose for us?

'This is the will of God, your sanctification' (1 Thessalonians 4:3, RSV). Paul is talking in this passage about how we 'ought to live and to please God' (4:1). He then outlines basic principles of behaviour by which we can judge individual matters. These are the 'instructions we gave you through the Lord Jesus' (4:2). Obedience to these moral instructions is for Paul the test of whether we are walking in the Spirit or disregarding the Holy Spirit.

As we look for guidance we see that there is an overriding principle that God's will for us in every matter is that we should grow in holiness, to be more and more like the Lord himself. 'But just as he who called you is holy so be holy in all you do . . . "Be holy, because I am holy".' The New Testament constantly repeats this idea that we should be holy. One way of finding God's guidance then is to ask the question: what would the holy Lord Jesus do in this matter? If we base our reactions, words and deeds on the pattern and character of the Lord, we won't go far wrong. Likewise we shall study the Scriptures and learn from them what sort of thing is pleasing to the Lord, so that we can base our lives on the teachings of the Bible.

1 Peter 1:15–16

'I chose you and appointed you to go and bear fruit' (John 15:16). Here we see a two-fold purpose in God's calling of us. He has appointed us to go and to bear lasting fruit.

When Jesus called his twelve disciples it was not only 'that they might be with him' but also 'that he might send them out to preach'. Both in John and Mark the disciples are appointed by the Lord for an out-going, fruit-bearing ministry. They are 'sent out'; they must 'go'. In Mark 3 the necessary command to be with the Lord in

Mark 3:14–15

close fellowship forms the preface to their being sent out. If they are to go out and bear fruit, they need to spend time in intimate relationship with their Lord and in learning at his feet. Too often we Christians separate these two inseparable elements. Some of us are deep in our devotional relationship with the Lord, love

> ... spend time in intimate relationship ...

to rejoice in prayer, praise and worship; but then we may be quite weak in evangelism. Others of us may be dynamic in evangelistic outreach but know nothing of quiet meditation at the feet of Christ. The disciples are called to both functions.

It is of considerable significance that Jesus' disciples are not only called to live the life of God but also are sent out to preach the good news. We too are disciples of Jesus and he sends us out also. We do not need special guidance to assure us that we are to go out into the world in witness. We may need some guidance as to where we are to go and exactly what strategies of evangelism we are to adopt there, but we know from the Bible that we are called to go.

'. . . fruit that will last' (John 15:16). God's purpose for us is that we shall bear fruit. We may wonder what sort of fruit is referred to in John 15. Is it the fruit of people responding in faith to the witness of Christ through us? Or is it the fruit of the Spirit, that lovely catalogue of spiritual qualities which we shall manifest if the Holy Spirit is at work in us? Perhaps it is both.

Gal. 5:22–23

Revelation 5:9

We are called to move out into all the world to bear fruit for Christ. The New Testament emphasizes God's saving purposes for all nations. The ultimate goal of our life and witness is that people 'from every tribe and tongue and people and nation' may worship the Lord. God's guidance for our individual lives should fit into his overall purposes for the world. We are not just individuals; we are also part of the history of God's church throughout the world and throughout history.

Gal. 5:18

Our out-going witness to the world needs to be linked to the fruit of the Spirit as listed in Galatians 5. These beautiful characteristics of holiness are the result of being 'led by the Spirit' – so the guidance of the Spirit cannot be divorced from living a life with the fruit of the Spirit. We are not only to come into the experience of life in Christ by the Spirit, but we are also to go on into the daily experience of walking by the Spirit. Spirit-led guidance will lead us into the fruit of the Spirit.

Gal. 5:25

And again, we are reminded that John says that this fruit should abide. God is not interested in mountain-top experiences which do not last. May God give us a holiness of character which lasts and which grows! We may judge a true work of the Spirit by what it produces five or ten years hence. When it is God who leads us, he never leaves a job half-done.

God is not interested in mountain-top experiences

When he is our guide, he takes us through every testing to the end.

So we see that there are overall principles concerning God's guidance, but these do not always include specific leading for every occasion. Just sometimes God may see fit to give more detailed guidance. Thus for the building of the temple God gives very specific instructions concerning every detail of the construction, leaving nothing to the free will of the builders. But this is not usually the case. At creation, God tells Adam and Eve to 'multiply and fill the earth and subdue it'. He commands them to have dominion over all the animals. But he does not fill in the details of how to accomplish these rather general commandments. Likewise the Old Testament gives wise overall principles concerning social behaviour in the state of Israel, but many details of daily economic and agricultural life are left to the discretion and wisdom of the   people. God gives us considerable freedom of scope for individual

... scope for individual self-expression ...

self-expression. He does not treat us as robots. He often trusts us to make responsible decisions on the basis of his overall purpose revealed in his word.

How do we know God guides?

God is very gracious to us and treats us all in an individual manner. He does not stereotype the way he guides us. He suits his guidance to our individual situation, character and background.

Choices

The prophets – tailor-made guidance. The call of Isaiah contrasts sharply with that of Jeremiah. God takes the highly gifted and self-confident Isaiah into the impressive temple building. Here the great Isaiah begins to feel how puny he really is! He is given a vision of the Lord himself

Isaiah 6:1 in majesty, 'high and lifted up'. Then he observes the flashing, burning seraphim flying about in the temple and calling to each other, 'Holy, holy, holy . . .' As if all that were not enough, God then causes the whole building to shake from the foundations up and the house is filled with smoke. Any pride or sense of self-sufficiency in Isaiah is surely knocked out of him by this fearful combination of events! No wonder he says, 'Woe is me! . . . I am ruined! For I am a man of unclean lips . . .' For the golden-mouthed Isaiah all this is a necessary prelude to hearing the voice of the Lord speaking to him, calling and guiding him into a prophetic ministry. Isaiah has to learn that God walks with people who have 'a contrite and humble spirit' and his reviving and renewing work is also for

. . . highly gifted and self-confident . . .

Isaiah 57:15 those who are humble.

Unlike Isaiah, Jeremiah was lacking in self confidence. He had a low image of himself and his abilities. He was stalked by a depressing awareness that everyone was against him. Such a man would have been destroyed if God had led him into the temple for the sort of experience that Isaiah had. He would have had a breakdown. But God graciously guided him in a much more gentle fashion which was more suited to his nature. God's key word to Jeremiah was 'I am with you and will rescue you.'   e.g. Jer. 1:8, 29

With Ezekiel, God's word came in the form of strange visions. God matches the forms of his speaking to our personality and character. Not everyone would appreciate the apocalyptic vision given to Ezekiel. But Ezekiel realized that somehow this 'was the appearance of the likeness of the glory of the Lord' (1:28). This caused him to fall prostrate before the Lord and then to hear the Lord actually speaking. Is this a pattern for guidance? When we are deeply conscious of God's overwhelming glory and fall in awe and humility before him, then we are in a right position to hear God speaking to us.

Is this a pattern for guidance?

God met Amos while he was busy in his daily work as a shepherd. As Amos says, 'the Lord took me from tending the flock' (7:15); Amos was 'one of the shepherds of Tekoa' (1:1). And the Lord suited his message to Amos' background and his prophecies are full of earthy agricultural imagery.

Both with Amos and Habakkuk God's word seems to have come in some visible form. Amos 1:1 talks of the words which the prophet saw. And Habakkuk 1:1 says 'The oracle of God which Habakkuk the prophet saw' (RSV). It is true that the Hebrew word for 'oracle' is rather uncertain in its meaning and may well have the sense of 'burden'. Habakkuk saw the burden which lay heavily on the very heart of God and in the following verses the prophet utters a cry to the Lord which echoes God's own heart cry. So the call of Habakkuk comes by seeing into the mind and feelings of God. His ministry then fits into that understanding. When we really grasp the heartfelt purposes of God, we are called to align our lives to them. God's leading then comes through this understanding of the mind of God.

It seems to make no sense ...

God suits his leading and calling to us as individuals. Guidance is not always easy to describe. I personally do not find it easy to say how the Lord has led me in different situations in my life. One can rationalize his guidance and over-simplify it, but actually one knows that all sorts of factors played a part in the fact of God's guidance.

For this reason, I have been much impressed by the beginning of Jeremiah and Joel – 'the word of the LORD came to me'. The Hebrew actually means 'the word of the Lord *was* to me'. It is meaningless in Hebrew, as it is in English. We want to ask immediately *what* the word was to Jeremiah or Joel. It seems to make no sense just to say that the word *was* to the prophet. But surely that is just the point. When we try to describe how the Lord's word of guidance or call really became clear, it seems so complex, and yet it came

Jer. 1:4; Joel 1:1

All descriptions seem trite and over-simplified

with assurance. We know the Lord has spoken to us, but all descriptions of how he led us seem trite and over-simplified. Often we just have to come back to this somewhat unsatisfactory biblical idea that the word of the Lord *was* just to me. Bad grammar may sometimes be good spiritual truth!

From the experience of the prophets, then, we can see that God suits his methods of guidance to the situation of his servants. Don't expect *your* guidance to come just like someone else's!

So let's look further at some of the many ways God led other people in the Bible.

Exodus – one step at a time. If we look at the book of Exodus, we see God leading Moses and guiding his people out of slavery in Egypt through the years of wandering in the wilderness and on towards the promised land of Israel. In chapter 2 comes the story of how Moses' sister was given wisdom in how to get the baby Moses back to the care of his mother. She had hidden him from the murderous designs of the Egyptians and concealed the baby in the bulrushes. In this story there is no mention of God at all. God allowed Moses' sister to use her own sharp mind and wise common sense.

...miracles alone are not enough

In contrast to this, we have the following chapter with the story of the burning bush. Here God begins his guidance through the miraculous sight of a bush burning without being consumed, but goes on to speak directly in a conversation with Moses.

In Exodus 5 Moses and Aaron become God's instruments to bring God's word of direction to Pharaoh. They pass on to him the Lord,s word that he should let Israel go. But Pharaoh points out that he does not know the Lord and will not Exodus 5:2 heed his voice. Then God speaks to Pharaoh through the series of plagues which he miraculously causes to fall on Egypt. But miracles alone are not enough. Pagan magicians can also do miracles – and the wise men of Egypt did in fact match many of Moses' miracles. Still today animistic spirit mediums, Hindu priests and the leaders of some Muslim mystical movements perform healings and other miracles. God does use miracles to introduce us to his word, but miracles alone are not an infallible evidence of truth.

We today can look back at the story of Israel's journey through the wilderness to Canaan, but at the time the people could only see one step at a time. In Exodus 17:1 they 'set out . . . travelling from place to place as the Lord commanded'. God often leads us in this way. We cannot see beyond the next step. Israel found this very difficult and Exodus 17 continues with Israel faithlessly complaining in rebellion against God and Moses.

When we were called together to missionary service in Indonesia, we assumed we would stay there until old age. After less than three years, we returned to our home country for home assignment and then the Indonesian political situation prevented us from going back there. God moved us on to Malaysia and then to Singapore. In the same way we had assumed that our call to serve with the OMF in Asia was for our lifetime. In fact, after ten years it proved right to move on to our present work at All Nations Christian College. Guidance is sometimes like driving without knowing the route, but being guided by someone in the passenger seat. They instruct you to follow the signs to some town and you think you must be going to that town. But after a while they redirect you to some other place. And so it goes on until you reach your actual destination. God may lead us by stages, one step at a time.

...in rebellion against God ...

So far, we have seen some fundamental principles of guidance illustrated in Exodus. We also note that God spoke often in an audible voice to Moses. He led Israel too in the visible form of the pillar of cloud and fire. We are bound to ask then whether God still guides us normally in such clear, tangible fashion. Christian mystics like Margaret Kempe have traditionally talked of the outward and the inward ear. Sometimes God may speak audibly so that we actually hear him with our ears, but normally we hear his directions through the inward ear of our conscience, our mind or our intuition. The very overt forms of guidance which were normal to Moses seem to be less common today. Perhaps Moses and the Old Testament saints needed this more

...even today God may lead his people in overt ways

specific guidance. They did not have the full Bible as we have it today, but just some oral traditions concerning the dealings of God with their forefathers.

Moses had relatively little understanding of the nature of God. Only in Exodus 6 did he first come to know the gracious covenant name of God *Jehovah* and it was even later that he was given the Law which is a lamp to our feet and a light to our path. But still it is clear that even today God may lead his people in overt audible or visible ways. If he sees that we need such clear and direct guidance, he can grant what we in our weakness may need. It does not seem, however, that this is the norm now.

Psalm 119:105

Acts – natural and supernatural. In the Acts of the Apostles God guides his people in a whole variety of ways. And sometimes the apostles simply proceeded without direct guidance from God so that it is just recorded that they did this or that. This is underlined by such words as 'he determined to return' or 'intending to' do something.

Acts 20:3
Acts 20:7, 13

As with Jesus, so with the apostles, their movements were often determined by what was their normal practice. In Acts 17:2 Paul follows his master's footsteps and starts his ministry in Thessalonica by going to the synagogue 'as was his custom'.

Sometimes guidance came through other people. But it was not always leaders who did the sending. In Acts 17:10 'the brethren' sent Paul and Silas away to Beroea. In 15:36–41 Paul and Barnabas both had ideas of what they wanted to do.

Circumstances played a vital part. Through persecution the Christians were scattered throughout Judea and Samaria, preaching God's word. It was through Jewish opposition and Gentile openness to the word that Paul and Barnabas were moved to begin preaching to Gentiles rather than Jews only. This was confirmed to them by their knowledge of the scriptures. Acts 8:1

Acts 13:44–46

Acts 13:47

But the book of Acts does also tell of direct guidance by the Holy Spirit. So in 13:2 and 16:6 the Holy Spirit speaks directly. In 8:26 and 27:23 it is an angel that speaks. It would seem however that there is a close connection between the angel and the Spirit, for the guiding word of the angel in 8:26 is immediately followed by the Spirit speaking to Philip in 8:29.

... guidance comes also through sensational means ...

Sometimes in Acts guidance comes also through more sensational means. Dramatic visions are given to Peter in Acts 10, to Paul in 16:9 and to Ananias at the conversion of Paul in 9:10. In 18:9 the Lord again speaks to Paul in a vision. We notice in 16:10 that the vision to 'come over to Macedonia and help us' evidently needs some discerning understanding, for they 'conclude' or 'infer' that God is calling them to preach the gospel there. It is apparently not immediately obvious. They have to think the vision through and interpret it.

In counselling with students at All Nations who have been given visions, I have sometimes noted that the vision may not be literally fulfilled, but it sets the student moving in certain directions.

In the New Testament church there were some people with a specific calling to be prophets. They played a part in the giving of God's guidance. In Acts 13:1 it was prophets and teachers through whom the Holy Spirit spoke to call Paul and Barnabas for special missionary work. Then in 21:10–14 there is the strange story of the prophet Agabus who foretells Paul's sufferings if Paul insists on going up to Jerusalem. This leads the Christians to beg Paul not to go, but he pays no attention to the prophecies and confidently asserts that he is ready to die for Jesus. Paul knows that God has called him to go to Jerusalem and will not allow himself to be turned aside from God's call. But doubtless, Agabus' prophecy would remind him that his sufferings in Jerusalem and then in Rome were within God's purposes for him and under God's control.

One guide – different voices

God does carefully lead us through life

God's methods of guidance vary according to the situation and to the person being guided. He graciously matches his dealings with us to our needs. We must not try to narrow down God's amazingly diverse patterns. We should also be careful not to consider one way of guidance more 'spiritual' than another. God may lead some of us in overt and dramatic fashion; others he may expect to use our sanctified common sense and our fundamental knowledge of Scripture. This may also vary from one stage of our Christian life to another. But whatever may be the methods of his guidance, we rest in the confident assurance that God does carefully lead us through life. He is our Father and our shepherd.

OVER TO YOU

1. What is your experience of a Father? How does this influence your view of God as Father and his guiding your life?

2. How can we develop a Christian mind-set? Be specific.

3. Can you identify with one of the prophets? If so, read again Isaiah 6, Jeremiah 1 or Ezekiel 1 and apply it to yourself.

4. List the ways God gave guidance in the Acts of the Apostles.

Three

Guidance and the Bible

The Christian Union meeting was over. Coffee loosened the tongues of the students as they stood around chatting together. A little group gathered round me with questions.

'At the end of this year, I finish my time here,' one said, 'and I have no idea what I should do next.' Another student chipped in: 'Yes, it's so difficult to know what God wants us to do. I've only been a Christian six months and I don't know what to do about my girlfriend. She's very tolerant about my becoming a Christian, but she doesn't want to have anything to do with Christians or Christian ideas. I like her a lot, but . . .' His words drifted into a silence which spoke eloquently of his deep uncertainty.

'Yes, but it isn't only those big decisions,' commented another person. 'As a Christian you want to do the Lord's will in all things, but how do you know what is to God's glory in the little decisions of everyday life?'

I don't know what to do about my girlfriend

How encouraging to see the keen determination of these young Christians to please the Lord in all things! I sympathized so much with their longing for quick and easy solutions to the whole question of guidance.

> ...how do you know what is to God's glory?

I began to tell them about our marriage relationship. In the early days, we loved each other very much but actually didn't know intimately how the other one ticked. Sometimes therefore we failed to do what our partner would really have liked. But our relationship in love was more important than the details of what we did or didn't do. Sometimes we needed to say to each other, 'I love it when you . . .' or 'I find it annoying when you . . .' But gradually we have grown to know each other more fully and we feel instinctively what would please or displease.

Words and the Word

'But that is precisely the point,' one of the students exclaimed with some impatience. 'How can we get to know God in such a way that we do appreciate what he wants in a particular situation?'

'Well, I suppose the Bible . . .' began another person, only to be interrupted quickly by a woman wearing very fashionable clothes. 'The

> ...longing for quick and easy solutions...

Bible is great, but you can't get life from a book. Words, words, words – the world is full of words! But you can't trust words. You can twist words to make them mean whatever you want. Surely God has got some better way than just words?'

I began to explain that actually God does use words, but not in a dishonest way. Right from the outset of history God has acted through words. It was when God spoke that creation took place. In Genesis 1 it comes again and again, 'God said, "Let there be . . .".' And when God spoke, things happened. John's Gospel picks up this theme when it says, 'In the beginning was the Word.' It also states that all things
John 1:3 were created through the Word. It was actually
John 1:4 in and through the Word that there was life. In fact John boldly equates the Word with God himself. So we have to be careful not to denigrate words, for God himself is identified with 'the Word'. And God creates through his Word.

Some people say, 'What's in a word?' and the answer surely must be that *words bring results*. This is especially true of God's 'word', the Bible.

Words and God's will. God's word is creative and active. It is also a word that reveals. The Old Testament is full of references to God speaking to his people and to his prophets. 'Thus says the Lord'; 'the Lord said to him . . .'; 'the word of the Lord came to me, saying . . .' Again and again God speaks to

> When God spoke, things happened

people in order to reveal his character and nature as well as his desires and purposes. These words became part of the writen word of God, the Bible. God himself wrote the Law on tablets which he then gave to Moses to bring down to the people of Israel.

God caused his revelation of himself in word and in historical actions to be recorded in the written word of the Bible. This written word became the ultimate authority in all matters and the source of a true understanding of God and his ways.

Words and the character of God. Through study of the Bible we learn the nature of our God. We then submit all uncertain questions to the test. Is this idea in line with what we know of the character of God? Is this course of action likely to please God and bring honour to him? Does this form of worship fit what we know of the holiness and grace of God? Through the Bible we grow in our understanding of the Lord himself. This then enables us to know whether a particular doctrine, form of spirituality or course of action would please him.

> ...the source of a true understanding of God

Our guidance is based primarily on God's self-revelation in the Bible rather than almost magically subjective bits of guidance. We shall look in a later chapter at subjective guidance which can also play a part in showing us God's will for us, but it will always be subject to

Scripture and so to our overall knowledge of the character of God.

I want to emphasize this fact that guidance is based on the knowledge of the character of God. Perhaps I can best do so by contrasting the ideas of revelation in Islam and Christianity. In Islam, revelation is fundamentally aimed at showing the will of God rather than helping people to know God himself. Islam does define certain characteristics of God in the so-called '99 most beautiful names of God', but there is also a strong sense that God is infinitely glorious, high above humanity and powerful. He is therefore above all description. He is also so removed from us that we cannot really relate to him intimately, like a child to a father. The aim of revelation is then to tell people what God wants them to do in worship, prayer and service. It is sometimes said that the *Qur'an* is like a signpost telling us the way.

Christianity is so different

Christianity is so different. God's word not only reveals the will of God, but above all it shows us God himself in order that we may know him, love him and worship him. This will of course result in joyful obedience and service because we are grateful to him for all he is and all he has done for us. Because we know him, we can also know his will for us. It is that way round.

Hear the word

So God's written word is our authority in all matters. What is not clearly found in Scripture cannot be authoritative. The Bible alone has authority over us. All forms of subjective guidance must be submitted to the test of Scripture. Even the guidance of Christian leaders does not have ultimate authority. And although we are not to be rebellious Christians who easily reject the words of our leaders, we

> ...put their words to the test

are to put their words to the test of Scripture and thus to our knowledge of the nature of God himself. Christian leaders will surely play a part in our guidance. But they do not have final authority over us and we must not just follow blindly what they say. Guidance comes from our knowledge of the Bible above all else.

Words and pictures. Some people react to such an emphasis on the Bible because they say 'The Bible is just words. You can't trust words.' After all Jesus used visual aids to get across his teaching. He instituted the visible symbols of bread and wine.

> ...visible symbols of bread and wine

Yet words are essential to *explain* the meaning of signs. And it should be added that even signs in the Bible have been handed down to us through the written words of the Bible. Even the Jewish

Passover tradition needs words. Jews share the Passover meal in their families with many symbolic actions and special foods which have significance. But during the meal the story of the original Passover is retold and thus passed down from generation to generation.

In the Christian Lord's Supper the symbolic eating and drinking of bread and wine means little without verbal teaching on the sacrificial death of Jesus.

God may therefore use other means of speaking to us beside words, but his primary method is through his word. This impresses us in the New Testament. Jesus and the apostles use words to show people God and his ways. Old Testament passages and verses are the proof of truth. As we have seen, when Paul makes his dramatic decisions to begin mission among Gentiles, he supports the rightness of this by Acts 13:46–47 quoting words from Isaiah.

The key word. But the New Testament is not just talking about the use of words to show people God and his will for us. The key to the New Testament is Jesus himself. And he does not just speak words – he *is* the Word. How can we play down the significance of words when our Lord himself is the Word? Let's be careful before we swallow slogan thoughts like 'actions speak louder than words'. God reveals himself in the person of the Word, Jesus the Messiah. Through this living Word we can know the John 1:18 Father – Jesus 'has made him known'. 'He who John 14:9 has seen me has seen the Father.' Through Jesus, the Word of God incarnate, we can so know the

Father that we shall understand his will. Jesus follows the will and purposes of God the Father. John 5:30; 6:38 If we base our lives on the example of Jesus, we too shall not stray from God's desires for our lives.

The word of God creates and reveals. It is 'living and active . . . discerning the thoughts and Hebrews 4:12 intentions of the heart'. And what does Paul say about the Scriptures in 2 Timothy 3:16–17? They are 'useful for teaching, rebuking, correcting and training in righteousness, so that the man of God may be thoroughly equipped for every good work'. What is guidance? Surely, it must include teaching, reproof, correction, training in righteousness and being equipped for the good works which God wants in our lives.

The word of God, incarnate and written, forms the basis of our Christian lives. If we want to know the will of God in any situation, we shall examine the example and teaching of Jesus as recorded in the Bible. We shall also study the whole Bible, the written word of God, to learn what

> . . . learn what pleases God and what arouses his anger

pleases God and what arouses his anger. On the basis of biblical teaching, we may then make sound decisions, praying that God's Spirit will help us to apply the Scriptures and the principles of the Bible to our particular situation. So how can we do that?

Making sense of the Bible

Get it in context. 'Wives, submit to your husbands as to the Lord . . . the husband is the head of the wife as Christ is the head of the church.'

Eph. 5:22–23 These verses are sometimes quoted to support a chauvinistic male domination in the home. Such a misuse of the verses not only fails to understand the real meaning of 'head' and 'submit', but it also takes these verses out of context. Paul goes on to show in what way Christ related to his bride, the church. He so loved the church that he sacrificially 'gave himself up for her'. This passage is not talking about male supremacy, but of mutual subjection. The husband does not lord it over a submissive wife, but follows the example of Christ in being her 'suffering servant'. If taken out of context, Bible verses can cause problems.

When we use a Bible verse, we should check its context.

Find the true sense. We were listening to a cassette about the life of Samson. The speaker on the cassette recounted how Samson only regained his strength when his shaven head grew a new crop of hair. The cassette applied this story to us today. If the church develops new forms, it will manifest the power of God. New songs, new forms of worship, new structures in the people of God; these are the essential conditions for new power by the Spirit.

> ...out of context, Bible verses can cause problems

We smiled at each other at this point. 'No,' I said, 'this passage tells us that the church lost its power when it allowed the old forms to be shaved off. We must put away new songs and other modern innovations. When the old hair is allowed to grow again, then we shall have power.'

...we may be seriously led astray ...

We laughed. Neither interpretation related at all to what Judges 16 is really talking about. Such use of Scripture is dangerously fanciful. We must stick to the true sense of a passage. Otherwise we may be seriously led astray in our personal lives and in the development of our churches and fellowships.

When we come to the Bible, we must always ask what this section of Scripture really means. What did the author intend to convey? What did the original readers centuries ago understand the passsage to mean? Only when we have asked such questions can we look to the Holy Spirit to apply the words to us and our situations today. We need to be very careful of a fanciful or allegorical use of Scripture.

Get behind the scenes. In Islam, the *Qur'an* is said to have been written by God on a tablet in heaven before all time. The *Qur'an* is the uncreated and eternal word of God. Its contents are not formed in any way by the prophet, nor are they culturally conditioned at all. Such theology is radically different from the Jewish and Christian belief. Our Bible is not only inspired by the Spirit of God, but also written by people in particular cultural and historical contexts. As we read any particular book of the Bible, we immediately notice this. For example, we may compare the book of Jeremiah with Luke's writings in his Gospel and Acts. It would be ludicrous to suggest that Jeremiah might have written Luke's Gospel or that Luke might have penned the prophecies of Jeremiah. They are written in different languages – clearly aimed at different people and coloured by the personal character of their authors.

Literalism may lead us into trouble ...

'The Bible says . . .' is not necessarily an infallible guide in life. We sometimes need to look at the background of a verse and see what it meant in its original cultural context. 'If your hand or your foot causes you to sin, cut it Mt. 18:8–9 off . . . if your eye causes you to sin, gouge it out.' I observe that a literalistic understanding of this verse is not popular even to those who claim always to follow the 'plain sense of Scripture'! How few blind Christians without hands or feet there seem to be! Literalism may lead us into trouble in our Christian lives.

With this in mind, we need to come again to some of the controversial issues of church life. Should women cover their heads when praying? Should women be allowed to preach, teach or pray aloud in public? What does the Bible teach about ordination by the laying on of hands? Or about tithing? Or about a day of rest on the Sunday?

Our lives are to be guided by God's revelation in the Bible. To achieve this we need to do our biblical homework seriously. Biblical passages should be kept in context, understood in their true sense and not fancifully. We then want to try to discover the significance of biblical teaching in the light of the cultures and ways of thought of biblical times.

Logos and *rhema* – a double act

'The Bible only gives us general principles of behaviour. It does not really tell us what to do day by day. We need more specific guidance than that. God should tell us clearly whether this particular person is his chosen partner for us. Should we apply for this work or training course? That is the sort of guidance which is important.'

'The Bible is only a book. A book-religion lacks real life. Paul says that the written word kills. It is the Spirit who gives life. For guidance, 2 Cor. 3:6 as indeed for every side of the Christian life, we have gone beyond just the Bible. We have the Spirit.'

Such quotes highlight a grave danger in the church today. The unique place of the Bible as the supreme revelation of God and of his will, yields ground to other more subjective forms of guidance.

Some Christians today are making a false distinction between two Greek words used in the bible for 'word'. *Logos* is thought to mean the ultimate, objective word which stands above everything, *rhema* is said to be the more living, direct word. *Logos* may therefore be the ultimate test of orthodoxy and truth, but it lacks immediate relevance and life. *Rhema* is both inspired and inspiring. It speaks directly to us and to the actual needs of the moment.

Logos, such people believe, is of course the word of God found in Scripture. *Rhema*, they think, may take various forms. It may be a verse or passage of the Bible which the Holy Spirit particularly highlights and brings to life in order to speak to us. It may also be a word of prophecy or a word of knowledge quite separate from Scripture.

But if *rhema* is the living word of God apart from Scripture, then the Bible in practice takes second place in our lives.

However, in the New Testament itself *logos* and *rhema* seem interchangeable. If, for example, we look at Luke 4:22, 32, 36 the direct speech of Jesus is said to be *logos*. His words (*logoi*, verse 22) are 'gracious' as he describes his own future ministry in Luke 4:18–19. Then in Luke 4:32 his *logos* astonishes his hearers because it is 'with authority' – surely then not some remote or unrelated objective word! And then in Luke 4:36 the *logos* of Jesus commands the unclean spirits and casts them out. It is not only in Luke that the *logos* of Jesus has direct miraculous power. In John 4:50 an official's son is healed by the powerful *logos* of Jesus.

On the other hand *rhema* stands not only for a direct prophetic word of power, but also for the gospel in general. In John's Gospel it is *logos* which creates all things, while in Hebrews 1:3 *rhema* upholds the whole universe. The New Testament includes dozens of references both to *logos* and *rhema*. Anyone taking the trouble to

1 Peter 1:25

look at the New Testament usage of these two words will see immediately that there is no distinction between them.

It sounds spiritual to contrast the objective word of Scripture with the dynamic living word applied to specific situations, but the Bible itself does not encourage this. The word of God, *rhema* and *logos*, reveals the character of God *and* his will.

Bible verses for you

In the old days some Christians picked a card out of their 'promise box'. On it was written a verse with a promise. Many have found

> Some picked a card out of their 'promise box'

guidance in this way. Later the 'promise box' gave way to the set verses of Daily Light. Or a calendar with a verse for each day hangs in the toilet to guide us through the decisions of the day. Other Christians may open their Bible at random and a verse leaps into focus – this must be the word of God for us today.

Such use of Scripture borders on magic. Dangers abound. We have to remember that the Devil also uses Scripture. Matthew 4:6–7 shows Satan and Jesus in spiritual combat, both using biblical verses as their weapon. In the question of guidance it is right that we should use verses from the Bible as our means of discovering God's will, but we must not assume that the Bible can be used like some book of magic formulas. We should check that Bible verses are kept in context and in their true meaning. And we shall want to compare the guidance a verse gives us with the overall teaching of the Scriptures.

At various times in my life I have found God leading me through a verse of Scripture. I was not expecting or looking for a verse to speak to me, but the Spirit made a word from the Bible stand out. These were memorable and exceptional occasions at times of particular need. At one time I had been fighting God's call to missionary service overseas. At another I felt God was stopping us returning to Indonesia because he had something else in store for us.

Dangers abound

God used a Bible verse to speak to us in a special way on another occasion too. We were in Indonesia at the time. The communists were very strong in their opposition to us. They picked on something I had said in a church elders' meeting and determined to take us to court for high treason. The penalty for this would be life imprisonment. The Indonesian legal system was terribly corrupt in the early 1960s and we knew we stood no chance of a fair trial. And our local prison was no holiday centre! It had no running water and prisoners did not normally have the chance to wash or use a toilet. The smell was indescribable. I lost my peace as I contemplated a lifetime

...determined to take us to court for high treason

in such a situation. I could not sleep. My mind went round and round without any rest. Prayer seemed futile.

In my distress God spoke. One morning I read Psalm 125:2. 'As the mountains are round about Jerusalem, so the Lord is round about his people.' If the Lord protects Jerusalem, no enemy can penetrate the wall of mountains around her. Was this not also so for me? I desperately asked the Lord to be like a range of mountains around me. From that day the communist party just forgot about their planned accusation against me. The whole affair slipped away.

God may indeed speak to us and guide us by Bible verses.

...no chance of a fair trial

Bible verses for groups

Guidance does not only come to individuals, but also to groups of Christians together. A verse of Scripture may also take on significance for a whole church. I remember a few years ago our college principal started the academic year with the verse 'the glory of the Lord filled the house'. For all of us on the staff and among the students this verse became the Lord's word to us and the theme of our prayers. As a college we longed that God's glory might so fill our buildings that even casual visitors would sense God's presence. We were much encouraged when various visitors and students' parents commented

1 Kings 8:11

Choices

God had led us
...to know what
to pray for

that they could feel God's presence as soon as they entered the front hall. God had led us as a college to know what to pray for.

God's word 'is a lamp to my feet and a light to my path'. Psalm 119 teaches us that God's word shows us the right way in which we are to walk. It asks how young people can keep their way pure and affirms, 'by guarding it according to your word' (verse 9). By storing up the word of the Lord in our hearts, we can be kept in God's ways of purity and preserved from the sin of false decisions (verse 11). The key to guidance is found in the Bible.

Psalm 119:105

OVER TO YOU

1. What can we do to encourage more understanding of how to interpret the Bible in our church or Christian Union?

2. What can we do to deepen our own personal knowledge of the Bible?

3. Has God used a Bible verse to guide your Christian Union? Look at that verse again and study it in its context. Does it still guide you in the same way?

Four

Subjective Guidance

'I felt the Lord was saying to me that I should . . .' 'The Lord led me to . . .' 'I knew this was God's word to me'. 'God called me to . . .' How often I have heard testimonies which have included such statements! The obvious question is, 'How?'

We noted in chapter 2 that God varies his guidance according to our individual character and situation. He guides in many different ways and it is impossible to categorize his methods too neatly. In practice, we find that God does not only speak to us through his word, the Bible. He has many different ways of showing us what his will is. But it must be constantly underlined that all subjective forms of guidance should be submitted to the test of Scripture.

> The obvious question is 'How?'

Get the message – God does guide

Before we begin to look at specific ways in which God leads us, it is good to remind ourselves first of the glorious truth that we can trust God to lead us step by step in his ways. We need the guiding hand of God, for otherwise we shall surely go astray. Wayward sheep need the constant care of a shepherd.

...compromising or sinful activities ...

God alone knows what is best for us and he graciously leads us. He has perfect plans for our lives and longs to show us his will. And it is so reassuring to know that his will is 'good, pleasing and perfect'.

Romans 12:2

First, the will of God is good. God's predetermined plan for our lives is morally upright. He desires that we should be holy as he is holy. God's leading will never be morally questionable, nor will it lead us into compromising or sinful activities. Holiness is a fundamental characteristic of our God and it is a basic factor in his guidance of us. He wants us to grow in holiness.

Lev. 11:44–45
1 Peter 1:15–16

Second, the will of God is pleasing. In Victorian times, it was taught that God calls his people to sacrifice. He would generally insist on us doing what we least want. 'Death to self', was the motto. There was little emphasis on a God of love who delights to lavish good gifts on his children. Today in unhappy

...all sorts of unfortunate images

homes the title 'father' may conjure up all sorts of unfortunate images. But Paul reassures us that our heavenly Father's will for us is 'pleasing'. God is not an ogre.

Third, Paul reaches the triumphant climax. The will of God is 'perfect' – and in the purposes of God, there is nothing superior to perfection. 'Perfect' is perfect! God does indeed have a plan and purpose for our lives. And there is nothing better than God's will for us. So we can walk with God in confidence.

God is not an ogre

Paul shows too that God has made us and brought us to new life in Christ with a specific intention. We are to produce those good works which God planned for us 'that we should walk in them'.

Eph 2:10 RSV

Yes, there are quite specific things he calls us to do for him, for his church and for his world. It is not just an academic truth that God has a definite purpose and calling for each one of us. He now challenges us to set out on the pathway he has designed for us. At every stage of life, we need to discover what good works God has in mind for us personally and 'walk in them'.

Although Ephesians 2:10 clearly teaches that God has detailed plans for our lives, we may not always need specific guidance on every point. We need not look for clear guidance on which shirt we wear today. If we wrestle in prayer on every tiny decision in daily life, we shall end up with a nervous breakdown. God may give us a strong sense of guidance even on the tiniest decisions, but normally we can just walk in the Spirit and trust God to lead us according to his purposes. This is the life of faith.

Actually, of course, it sometimes happens that an apparently insignificant decision can have major repercussions. For example, I have a pullover from Peru of traditional Peruvian Indian design. One day, a group of young Peruvians saw me wearing it. Through this we soon got into conversation and I was able to share Christ meaningfully with them. As we walk with the Lord, he guides us even in tiny matters like the choice of which pullover to wear! We can trust him to guide us without us even sensing his direction in such matters.

But the more important the decision, the clearer we shall want to be about the Lord's will for us. For example, in the choice of a life partner.

How then does God make his will known to us on particular issues?

The mind of Christ

I love the verse in Philippians where Paul says Phil. 2:13 RSV that 'God is at work in you, both to will and to work for his good pleasure'. There are four stages in the action of this verse: God works in us; we want that which pleases him; we then do the work he wants; finally comes the climax that he gets pleasure from it all. But it all starts with God working in us and shaping our wills so that we long to please him. We begin to desire what he desires, to like what he likes. It is no longer a struggle between our selfish, proud aims and the gracious promptings of the Spirit. Our minds and our wills are attuned to what God wants.

When students ask me about guidance for the future, I often ask them, 'What would you really like to do?' If I get an answer which shows a selfish or

What would you really like to do?

materialistic outlook, then I want to challenge them to get right with the Lord before they worry too much about guidance. But if they are clearly wanting the will of the Lord and to live for his glory, then my question can be very helpful. 'I would love to work among Muslims in North Africa,' a bright young woman said to me recently, 'but am I the right sort of person for that? And I am not sure of God's

I did not want to be a missionary

call.' I suggested that it might be the Holy Spirit who was at work in her giving her that desire.

So I encouraged this woman to move definitely in the direction of missionary service in North Africa. God would confirm the rightness of it by giving her his peace. But if we were misreading the will of God, then he could easily close the door for her. If we genuinely want to obey him, God will not allow us to go astray.

It might be wise at this stage to add a small word of warning! When it comes to the question of boy/girl relationships, we need to be rather more cautious. In chapter 6, we shall look at some of the things we should look out for in guidance about a life partner.

The peace of God

In Colossians 3:15 Paul exhorts his readers, 'Let the peace of Christ rule in your hearts.'

I remember how I felt before God called me into missionary service. I was studying modern languages at university and people began to say to me, 'Keen Christian plus linguist equals missionary.' I felt their mathematics was false. Many Christians are keen on languages without necesssarily being called to overseas mission. I denied their logic. I did not want to be a missionary. God had not called me, I maintained.

But I began to lose my sense of peace with God. My prayer times seemed cold and unreal. As I considered the future, it lacked purpose and appeared unclear. Life lost its joyful vigour. God was showing me that I had wandered in my plans onto the wrong track. It was only when I realized God's call and surrendered to his will that God's peace returned to me.

...the future lacked purpose

Of course, we can lose our peace for other reasons. An undisciplined lifestyle with inadequate sleep can lead to headaches, mild depression and loss of peace. Purely physical problems may steal our peace from us – a persistent cold, nagging asthma or a bout of 'flu. Women may find that they temporarily lose their peace at a particular time of the month. When we talk of God's peace being a factor in guidance, we are not talking of such temporary and human matters. We mean a long-term and continuous lack of peace where God seems to be disturbing our nest and pushing us to fly in new directions.

We should not rush into a new calling without first testing this sense of loss of peace. Don't abandon your studies in your enthusiasm over a challenge to full time service. Don't walk out on your job because of bored dissatisfaction or some difficulty in relating to your boss. Don't flit from church to church in a search for the ideal spiritual fellowship. Butterflies don't make good Christian workers!

The peace of Christ in Colossians 3:15 is linked to the following verse: 'Let the word of Christ dwell in you richly'. The word for 'dwell' gives the idea of God's word making its home in us. So let the word of Christ richly indwell you. Let God's word in the Scriptures so fill you and permeate your thinking and your attitudes that God can then guide you by his peace.

Signs from above

Deserted army barracks surrounding a huge tent became the base for a linguistics course for missionary candidates. It was here that we

It was here that we first met

first met. We sat opposite each other the first evening at supper. I fell in love on the spot.

Elizabeth was the girl I wanted, but was this really God's will? We were both heading for missionary work with the same mission in the same part of the world. But I wanted to be sure of God's leading. I asked God to give me signs. 'Lord, let me meet her on my way to the kitchens' – and, sure enough, she happened to be there! 'Lord, arrange for us to be in the same class, if you really mean us to be together for life' – and so it worked out! In his grace, God gave me sign after sign to encourage me to persist in my love for Elizabeth.

It is rare in the Bible that God looks for his people to ask for a sign. There is no evidence in the New Testament of people asking for a sign but God may, however, give signs to confirm the reality of his work. In Luke 2:12 the shepherds were given the sign of 'You will find a baby wrapped in cloths and lying in a manger.' This confirmed to them that God had indeed sent the Saviour, the Lord and Messiah. So also in the early church, the truth and reality of their preaching was confirmed by signs and miracles. In Mark 16:20 it is clear that the signs follow after the disciples go out to preach the word. The signs were not a starting point for faith or guidance, but God gave them to demonstrate the spiritual authenticity of the words. The New Testament Christians do not

> ...was this really God's will?

seem to have asked for signs as a means of guidance.

We read in the Gospels and 1 Corinthians that the Jews frequently asked for a sign. Jesus rejected their demand and pointed out that it is an evil generation which wants a sign. 'Jews demand signs', but Paul affirms that he will only 'preach Christ crucified'. Paul refused to pander to their desire for signs.

Matthew 12:39
1 Cor. 1:22

Of course it is easier to know God's will if he will grant us concrete signs.

As I look back to those days when I asked for clear signs to confirm that Elizabeth was God's chosen partner for my life, I realize just how immature I was. Perhaps God saw that I was spiritually weak and immature, so I needed visible signs. In his grace God always gives us what we need.

> I realize how immature I was

Visions and dreams

In the Old Testament God frequently spoke to people and guided them by means of dreams.

Paul often received God's guidance through a vision, while Joseph and the wise men from the east saw dreams at the time of Jesus' birth. (The Bible seems to make little or no distinction between visions and dreams, e.g. Numbers 12:6.)

Does God still speak to people in this way? Yes! A young Scottish friend of mine was working by his machine on the factory floor one day

... one could not deny the reality of visions ...

when he suddenly saw a vision of Jesus telling him that he should become a missionary to Asia. My friend was not only converted that day, but set his face towards missionary service in Asia.

A few years ago I visited East Malaysia at a time of sweeping revival. It was challenging to be asked to discern the meaning of many dreams which people had received. Sometimes the message was clear, sometimes it seemed impossible to know what it meant. But one could not deny the reality of visions. Many Muslim converts have been drawn to Christ through a dream or vision.

It sometimes happens that a picture comes into our minds as we are praying or waiting on the Lord. Such pictures can be a beautiful gift from God to make his will clear to us. Of course, like all visions and dreams, pictures can come from three different sources – from God, from Satan or from our own natural minds. Visions call us to exercise the gift of discernment and should be particularly tested by the standards and teaching of the Bible. If the picture or vision leads us to unholy living or to unbiblical emphases in our teaching, it is certainly not from the Holy Spirit.

... pictures can be a beautiful gift from God ...

The Bible constantly warns us not to be unduly impressed by the spectacular. Even signs and wonders

Mark 13:22 can come from false prophets and may even lead the elect astray. And certainly dreams, visions and mental pictures are unreliable channels of God's guidance unless carefully tested by the standards and teaching of Scripture and the holy purity of God.

...tested by the standards and teaching of the Bible

Prophecy today

What exactly is prophecy? It may be a word from God foretelling the future. In the Old Testament it often did tell in advance the details of the coming of the Messiah, the judgment of the nations or some future event in history. But prophecy is also a message inspired by the Holy Spirit applied to particular needs or situations. It may be a word of rebuke, encouragement or exhortation.

Dreams and visions were part of the pentecostal fulfilment of the prophecy of Joel 2:28 and Acts 2:17 says that 'your sons and your daughters shall prophesy'. When God pours out his Spirit, we can expect that Christians will be inspired to prophesy. Prophecy is mentioned also in Romans 12:6, Ephesians 2:20, 3:5, 4:11 and Revelation 10:11. In 1 Thessalonians 5:20 Paul commands us, 'Do not despise prophesying.

And the ministry of prophecy did not cease with the writing of the New Testament but continued in the church for many years. The gift was particularly common in the churches of

...prophecy was no longer recognized in the church

the Middle East and among the monks and asce-
tics of Egypt and the desert areas.

But gradually the gift of prophecy was no
longer recognized in the church. Was this
because the church had lost its vitality? Or
does God only pour out on his people the gifts
he sees to be needed by them at any particular
time in history? It seems more likely, however,
that this spiritual gift was in fact practised
throughout Christian history, but not known
by that name. People may have called it
'inspired teaching/preaching' or 'a word from
the Lord' and failed to see that actually it was
prophecy.

I find this answer more acceptable than
to suggest that the church lacked spiritual vitality for so many centuries. I do not think that
we today are more spiritual than our forefathers!

Is prophecy God speaking?
Does prophecy hold the
same weight and authority
as Scripture then? Those
who emphasize the bibli-
cally untenable distinction
between *rhema* and *logos*
would tend in practice to
equate prophecy and Scripture as 'The Word of
God'. Thus Bruce Yocum in his book on prophecy states that prophecy is 'almost like listening
to a tape-recorded message'. Many feel that
prophecy is indeed God's very words relayed to
us. I query this. The Bible alone is God's perfect
word. Only in the Bible does God's Spirit so

> Was this
> because the
> church had lost
> its vitality?

inspire people and overrule their fallible human nature that their words are actually God's unadulterated word. Prophecy, like preaching and teaching, should be God-inspired, but the message still comes through the mediation of the speaker.

In Scripture we believe that this human mediation was so directed and overruled by God's Spirit that the Bible is God's perfect word. But I do not believe that this is the case with prophecy today. The sin and weakness of the speaker will distort and corrupt the message, so that it is fallible. The hearer will need therefore to use discernment in testing the message, sieving out the human corruption of God's message and then obeying what is seen to be God's word to us.

The impression that a prophecy is literally the direct words of God is enhanced by the use of the first person singular, as in the jargon formula, 'My little children, I . . .' It would be better to say, 'I feel that God is wanting to encourage/warn us that he . . .'

> . . . sieving out the human corruption of God's message . . .

If a prophecy comes in the first person singular, it seems that we dare not criticize it. God's own words are above discernment! Surely we can only humbly submit and obey. But if the prophecy comes in the more modest third person with the assumption that it comes through a fallible human being, then we can happily exercise discernment.

Choices

How can we tell it's true?

a) It must be in accord with the teaching of Scripture and the character of God revealed in the Bible and in the person of Jesus Christ.

b) It should lead to the hearer exalting the basic truths of the Christian faith.

c) Careful assessment by other Christians who are accustomed to speaking in a prophetic manner.

1 Cor. 14:29

d) The test that Jesus gave in Matthew 7:16: 'You will know them by their fruits.' Galatians 5:22-23 lists nine aspects of the fruit of the Spirit. A prophet's life should show holiness, spirituality and sound doctrine.

e) If a prophecy is predictive, then we should watch carefully to see if it is fulfilled. Some Christians have been excited by prophecies that the four million Soviet Jews will come out from Russia through Scandinavia to Israel. This would happen in the middle or late 1980s, some said. There has been a partial fulfilment in the exodus of some thousands, but it is only a small minority – and did not involve Scandinavia.

The genuineness of the prophet's gift will be seen in the fulfilment or non-fulfilment of his or her words. In the Old Testament the penalty for false prophecy was stoning. This may sound extreme. But to speak in the name of God is no light matter.

Who should discern prophecy?

a) Other people with prophetic gifts. In 1 Corinthians 14:29 Paul says, 'Let two or three prophets speak, and let the others weigh what is said.' It is very possible that this verse is suggesting that prophecy should be tested and discerned by other Christians who have the same prophetic gift.

b) All believers. Paul goes on to say that 'all can prophesy one by one'. He seems to be opposing the idea of some élite circle of people with a special prophetic gift. The whole body of Christians has the spiritual responsibility as well to judge whether a particular prophecy is a genuine word from the Lord.

> ...to speak in the name of God is no light matter

c) Church leaders. In some churches a Christian is not allowed to give a word of prophecy unless it has first been submitted to the church leaders. And yet all Christians are a 'royal priesthood' with direct access to the presence of God through the shed blood of Jesus. Because of the sacrificial death of Christ for our sins, we can all know God personally and intimately, hearing his voice to us and discovering his will. We must not surrender these precious privileges by making our leaders into mediators between God and ourselves. Jesus is our one and only mediator; we need no other, for he is totally adequate.

1 Peter 2:9

But Christian leaders do have the responsibility to set an example to their flock and to teach the word of God. They should therefore lead their people in the exercise of the gift of discernment, helping the congregation to test the biblical validity of prophetic words. In their leadership they should have the courage to say openly if for some reason they do not think a word of prophecy is genuine.

There is a particular problem here in groups of young or inexperienced Christians, such as school or college Christian fellowships or Christian Unions. The leaders may not be mature enough to shoulder this responsibility. In such cases Christians would be well advised to be particularly careful before naively accepting prophecies or visions. If problems still remain, it may be wise to call in a mature Christian leader for advice.

The relationship of prophecy to guidance is not easy. Clearly God does want to speak to us in relevant ways which apply to our particular situations. His main method of speaking is through the Bible. But he also uses prophetic preaching, teaching and Bible exegesis. Other prophetic utterances can play a part too in showing us the will of God when we face decisions.

Some Christians today are amazingly gullible in naively accepting so-called prophecies as God's word to them. Other Christians are so sceptical and critical that the Spirit may easily be quenched. The Christian walks on a tightrope.

Words of knowledge

The Spirit may also give us a word of knowledge in which he makes us aware of things we
could not otherwise know. It
is not easy to distinguish this
from a natural gift of wise
discernment, but it should be
said that the so-called 'natural' is also God's creative
work in us and therefore
need not be so separated
from spiritual gifts. Likewise, it is not always
easy to distinguish between a word of knowledge and just a hunch or feeling. This is particularly difficult if the word of knowledge or
hunch is not absolutely specific. 'Somebody in
the meeting tonight has toothache' – it is more
than likely in a good-sized meeting that there
will be somebody with toothache!

   In the exciting movement of God in Timor,
Indonesia, in 1965-68, Christians were told by
God to do evangelism in a particular village –
the name of which they had never heard of
before. Then they were told the name of the man
there whom they were to contact and to whom
they were to preach the good news of Jesus. It
was very specific.

Philip's story. In Acts 8 Philip was told to leave
Samaria and go to a desert road. Philip did not
hesitate to obey this somewhat subjective word
of guidance. We might deduce from this that God
looks for immediate and total obedience without
careful sifting when we hear a word of guidance.   Acts 8:27

> The Christian
> walks on a
> tightrope

But perhaps we need to notice various factors in the story before we apply it too quickly.

We know from Acts 6 that Philip had been chosen for the humble ministry of serving tables because he was a person 'of good repute, full of the Spirit and of wisdom'. He was therefore not Acts 6:3 only filled with the Spirit, but also morally upright and known for his wisdom. He had also shown his humble faithfulness by serving tables while others had the up-front preaching ministry. Such a person may readily discern the word of the Lord.

Philip was a person who so knew the word of the Lord and the mind of Christ that he was happy to go down to Samaria to preach to these non-Jews without any specific guidance at all. From his knowledge of Christ and the Scriptures Acts 8:5 he knew that the gospel should be preached not only to Jews, but also more widely to the Samaritans. Knowing that this was within the purposes of God he went down to Samaria without waiting for guidance. This was the sort of person who was able then to react immediately Acts 8:6–8 to the angelic word of guidance.

We notice that the angel's guidance led him away from the revival work of Samaria to the barren situation of the desert road. He was led away from the glamour of the crowds to the obscurity of a lone Ethiopian eunuch. How rarely subjective guidance today seems to lead us away from the spectacular and sensational to the unsung solitude of the desert!

... led away from the glamour of the crowds ...

OVER TO YOU

1. How can we know the difference between natural loss of peace and the divine umpire's work of guidance?

2. Study Colossians 3:12–17 and Philippians 2:1–13, putting Colossians 3:15 and Philippians 2:13 into context.

3. If you hear what claims to be a word of knowledge or prophecy, how do you judge/discern its message?

Five

Guidance and the Church

The barracks hummed with eager debate. The barriers between officers and men yielded to the uniting pressure of this major decision facing them. Should the whole battalion turn to Jesus Christ and be converted to the Christian faith? Most of the men were convinced that Jesus Christ could give them a new life which would transform the whole atmosphere of their army life.

...a general consensus of opinion emerges ...

But some objected. Some Muslim soldiers felt there could be problems with their families. Others were not sure that the Christian life fitted the rough-and-tumble of the army. All knew that they needed a new pattern of relationships. Finally the decision was taken. The way ahead was clear. Officers and men together submitted to the authority of Christ. As the poet Arthur Clough says, 'There is a great Field-Marshal, my friend, who arrays our battalions.' The whole battalion underwent instruction in the Christian faith and then gave their allegiance through baptism to their new commander.

What's in a group?

In many cultures overseas it is customary for decisions to be taken by groups of people together. The lock-stock-and-barrel conversion of this army battalion was not unique in Indonesia. I had the joy one day of leading a whole hospital ward to Christ. Soon after we left the country a senior school of five hundred teenagers was converted.

Such group decisions relate not only to conversion, but God's guidance may also come to groups of people together.

All of us in our families have indulged in such debates. Finally, a general consensus of opinion emerges and a decision is taken. If this group discussion takes place with prayer, surely God will lead us to the right decision by his Spirit. Committees work on this principle. Debate ranges around a matter until finally the Spirit leads to a communal decision. Is this what happened in Acts 15? Peter spoke first, followed by Barnabas, Paul and finally James. Finally 'it seemed good to the apostles and elders . . .' It had also been through a group decision that Paul and Barnabas had been set aside for wider missionary service in Acts 13:1–3. The Holy Spirit said: 'Set apart for me Barnabas and Saul . . .'

Acts 15:22

Some British churches today are doing something very similar. They see a town or housing estate with little live Christian witness and determine to plant a new church there. Church planting is better done by a team of Christians resident in the locality, so that local people can actually see the people of God living and worshipping together. The established church therefore separates several of its members to move house into the target area and start the new church.

Who decides which Christians should move house and start the new work of evangelism or church planting? Unless the church is exceedingly autocratic, it cannot simply tell people to move house and start a new church elsewhere. The people concerned will need to be consulted. They will then prayerfully consider the suggestions put to them before agreeing to them – or rejecting them!

'Guidance by consensus.' Guidance may come through the church as a body or through the leadership of the church, but it must then be checked by any individuals concerned.

In the mission to which my wife and I belonged we called this 'guidance by consensus'. Within the basic principle there was considerable room for flexibility. When we joined our mission in 1960 the emphasis was on guidance through the leaders. So they interviewed us when we first arrived in Singapore and then, after considerable prayer, tentatively designated us to work in a particular country. We were then asked to pray through their suggestion and hopefully put a tick to it.

...considerable room for flexibility

Today the emphasis has shifted. New candidates to the mission are asked to discover from the Lord where he wants them to work. This sense of call is then submitted to the leaders of the mission, who will agree it if at all possible. But there is still the same basic idea that the Lord leads both the individual missionary and also the leaders of the mission together.

If two agree

'Barnabas took Mark'; 'Paul chose Silas'; 'Paul wanted Timothy to accompany him'; 'the brethren sent Paul and Silas away by night'; Paul 'called to him the elders of the church'. It seems that *all* Christians at that time were open to receive their guidance through the mediation of other believers.

If two Christians agree in asking for something in prayer, then it will be given to them. Mt. 18:19 And if two or three are gathered in the name of Jesus, then he is specially present with them. So also in guidance there is the assurance of Jesus' Mt. 18:20 presence when Christians gather together. It is wise therefore for individual Christians to meet with other Christians when we face serious decisions.

This has two advantages. First, we are specially aware of the Lord's presence when we are in a group like that, so it seems easier to hear his voice and determine his will. Second, we find that each of us has different insights which can be added

... it seems easier to hear his voice and determine his will

together to bring combined wisdom to the situation.

I am often amazed how apparently very unclear situations have become so very obvious when we have come to the Lord in such groups together.

> ...very unclear situations have become very obvious...

A local church may have a pastoral committee to help members facing personal problems or a missionary committee to advise people who are wondering about Christian service overseas. Otherwise individual Christians may ask a few respected Christians who know him or her well. They may then meet together to discuss and pray about the situation in order that they may find the mind of the Lord.

It is of course wise to ask for such help from older and more experienced Christians who are known for their wisdom and sprituality.

Love your local church. When Christian leaders sense the Lord's guidance and feel that they are discerning the ministry which some Christian ought to begin to exercise, they should gently suggest this to the person. They will not presume to tell him or her that their suggestion is a definite word from the Lord which must be obeyed, but will tentatively put the proposition to the younger Christian and ask him or her to pray about it. In this way the will of God may be shown to a Christian through church leaders or other believers.

Individual Christians today will often face the situation of having various groups of leaders caring for them and offering them guidance. By force of circumstances we may belong to one church in our home town where our parents live, another in the place where we studied and a third where we now work. Students are often involved in CUs too, while missionaries have a responsibility to their society, sending church and national church.

...a definite word from the Lord

As Christians we may look up to older believers in each of these and they may play some part in guiding us in the name of the Lord.

It is easy to talk in theory of the responsibility of the church to see the gifts and talents of their members, to help guide them in the Lord's way and to stand prayerfully with them in these questions of guidance and pastoral needs. But suppose the church does not have the spiritual life or vision needed?

One of my students felt strongly that he should not go overseas as a missionary unless his home church felt it right and agreed to be his sending body. But they did not have that kind of vision. They had no interest in mission overseas and felt no pastoral responsibility of that sort for their members. Many of us feel it right to play our part in witness within a local church which is not overflowing with spiritual

...they did not have that kind of vision

life. We may not then be able to look to the church for help in guidance. Others of us may belong to churches which are too strong in their emphasis on authority and 'covering'. We may then face the tension between an unbiblical submission and a contrary independence of view which the leaders will not accept. Nevertheless we shall not want to slip into an individualism which does not allow us to find the Lord's will for our lives with the help of more senior Christians who know us well.

Don't go it alone

The rubber-tapper's dark little house stood at the end of the village on the edge of a large rubber plantation. The whole family had gathered together, the parents with their nine children plus grandparents, uncles and aunts. As pastor to the older children I too had been asked to attend this family gathering and give my opinion in the question to be debated.

> We don't have enough money to educate all the children

The father explained, 'We don't have enough money to educate all the children. The price of rubber is down. We can only afford now to have one child at school. The question before us is: which child?'

Everyone present shared their views and the final decision was clear to all. We were unanimous in asking the third child to continue at school, go on to university and study to become a doctor. The others left school the next day. One followed his father in tapping rubber, another became a petrol-pump attendant in a local garage.

From then on all watched the child at school. Today he is a fine Christian doctor, but who does his salary belong to? The family, of course! He owes everything to his family. How would the family react if he suddenly said he felt called to give up his career and become a missionary? Impossible! He cannot disregard the rights of his family and his responsibility to them.

Our guidance is never restricted to ourselves in its effects. The command of God does not say, 'honour your parents until you are eighteen or twenty-one'. We have the God-given duty to honour our parents even after we are mature adults. We cannot snap our fingers at our families, saying that we feel that God is guiding us in a certain way. We must always take our family into consideration.

> God does not say, 'Honour your parents until you are eighteen ...'

In seeking God's guidance we are not just looking for our own satisfaction. Of course it is true that God has given us our particular background, gifts, talents and personality. He surely wants these to be fully used – he gave them to us for a purpose. Nothing is accidental; God is sovereignly in control of our lives from the moment of our conception. He surely wants us to be fulfilled through the proper exercise of all our gifts, but we for our part should not be selfishly aiming at our own self-fulfilment.

As we pray for the Lord's will to be made clear, we have two aims in mind – to bring glory to the Lord and to serve the needs of others.

Our primary goal in life is to glorify the name of the Lord. The Christian is saddened by the way God's name and the name of Jesus are dragged in the mud. The Christian longs to make it clear what the Lord is like and what he has done for us, so that people will come to love him, believe in him and give him the honour which is his due.

'. . . and your neighbour as yourself'. Our secondary goal goes inseparably together with the first. If we love the Lord our God, we shall also love our neighbour as ourselves.

When we wonder about a career or look for a job, we shall ask ourselves and the Lord how best we can be used to serve a needy world. We shall not be asking the world's usual questions about promotion possibilities, salary scale, job satisfaction or career prospects; rather we shall be asking whether this job gives scope for service to the church and to society. When we consider where to set up home, we shall not ask which area is nicest or which house is the best we can afford. We shall not just look for a home near a church which can feed us and give us happy fellowship. We shall ask ourselves where we can be of most use to the Lord and the church of God. Where

> . . . how best can we be used to serve a needy world?

can we be of service to needy people in our society? This should be the basis for our guidance.

Fitting into God's great plan. As Christians, we do not believe that we live independently of others. We are part of the total body of Christ throughout all ages and all over the world. In our guidance we shall also take this into consideration. Surely the Lord will lead us in such a way that our lives and ministries fit into the overall pattern of his working through history and throughout the world. How can I fit my ministry into the overall strategy of God in the world?

What is God wanting to do today? When I was a student there was a great burden on many hearts for the continent of Latin America which was at that time a rugged mission field with little evangelical witness. Today the situation has markedly changed. We now face the formidable challenge of the world of Islam. How can we fit our lives into that call from the Lord to his church? What will be the supreme challenge of God to his people in the next generation? Southern Europe?

God does guide individuals. But our guidance must fit into God's working in the wider circles of the church and of the world. Guidance is not just selfish without due consideration of others.

Guidance together

God guides not only individuals, but also groups of people together. When he does guide individuals, he may well do so through the church and through the wise counsel of more mature Christians who know them well. God's guidance of the individual not only touches the life of that person, but also has wider ramifications. We have to consider our guidance in the light of our wider responsibilities – to our families, the church and its needs worldwide, and the world in its suffering and injustice.

OVER TO YOU

1. Which mature Christians could you turn to for help in questions of guidance? What natural and spiritual qualities make them suitable for this role? How well do they know you?

2. As you consider job applications, what motives are primary? List them in order of importance.

3. How could you best contribute to God's development of the history of the church worldwide? If you think this is too ambitious a question, what is your purpose in life?

4. How do you relate your personal sense of guidance to the wishes of your parents and family?

Six

Circumstances and Common Sense

The Bible comforts us with the strong message of God's sovereignty. He directs and controls the movements of the nations through history. His loving purposes graciously lead his people. He overrules the lives of individual believers.

We may expect therefore that he will so arrange our circumstances that we are gently pushed into the way he has planned for us. Sickness and physical weakness don't come by chance. The demands of infirm elderly parents are not accidental. Failure to find employment does not take God by surprise. God often uses such things to lead us in his way. When we are wondering about guidance, we should always take such circumstances into account, believing that our God reigns as Lord of all things.

> Sickness and physical weakness don't come by chance

Paul prayed that the Lord would open to him a door for the preaching of God's word and in Col. 4:3

Revelation 3:8 God assures his people 'I have placed before you an open door, that no-one can shut.' It is God who opens or closes doors for us. He often uses natural circumstances towards this end.

A Swiss friend of ours had felt the call of God to missionary work in Thailand for many years. She patiently completed her medical studies, had a couple of years of professional experience, started her missionary training – and then discovered that she had an incurable back complaint. The missionary society could not possibly accept her with such an illness. We had to face the possibility that it was Satan preventing her from such front-line service.

Failure ... does not take God by surprise

We prayed for her healing, but gradually the Holy Spirit gave us the sure conviction that God had other purposes for her.

She now has a rich and influential ministry in Switzerland, but her previous call to Thailand has given her a special love for that land. She prays fervently for others who work there. Her deep interest in Thailand is infectious, so God has used her to call others into missionary service there and into caring support in prayer and finance. And our friend's sufferings, as Paul affirms in Romans 5:3–5, have indeed produced in her a spirit of patient endurance, a depth of character and a confident hope in the Lord.

Open doors

...a depth of character and a confident hope

If God graciously opens a door for us, we should walk confidently through it into the paths he has planned for us. If God closes a door, we should not fret or complain, but joyfully rest in the assurance that the sovereign Lord knows what is best. We have noted before that his will is 'perfect'. It is not only true that God may use circumstances to lead us into his will for us. Equally he will confirm it through circumstances when we have made a decision in accordance with his purposes. 'We shall need a house; we have no furniture; what about our children's schooling? Our bank balance is nil; our parents need us; we surely won't be able to find a job there.' Our minds often go round and round worrying about all the problems. Sometimes it is hard to see how things will pan out, but the Lord is still in control. If we follow his leading, he will wonderfully make all our circumstances fall into place.

What if we go wrong?

Our minds go round and round worrying ...

But what happens if we make the wrong decisions? Do we have to walk through life with the depressing knowledge that we have missed God's best purposes for us? No! The sovereign Lord knows everything in advance.

He knew before the creation of the world what we would be like and what decisions we would take. He is well able to overrule all circumstances, including our mistakes and our sins to bring blessing. 'We know that in *everything* God works for good with those who love him.'

Romans 8:28

We have experienced the reality of this. Our missionary career seemed to go wrong at every stage! We were designated to serve in Indonesia, but no visa was forthcoming. As a result I gained invaluable experience in South Thailand. Then we had under three years serving in the Indonesian churches before political developments prevented us continuing our ministry there. Later we moved with joy to a training ministry in Singapore, but soon faced the bitter disappointment of being asked to relinquish that work after just three years. Our leaders felt we had been inadequate. We certainly had made mistakes. But with hindsight we can see now how God was moving us towards our present work and preparing us for it in his perfect, gracious way.

As the Psalms declare, 'the steps of a man are from the Lord'. He will keep our steps steady on the right pathway. We need not fear!

Psalm 37:23
Psalm 119:113

It is not only our outward circumstances which are under God's direction, but also the infinite and complex details of our background, personality and gifts. Our character and experience are given us by God for a purpose. As we face guidance decisions we should sensibly take into

Our leaders felt we had been inadequate

account these vital factors – what sort of people has God caused us to be? What training and experience has he led us into? He makes no mistakes.

The prophet Jeremiah had to learn this. In calling him to be a prophet God reassured him that 'Before I formed you in the womb I knew you, before you were born I set you apart.' God determined to call Jeremiah to a prophetic ministry even before he was born. But Jeremiah still demurred and made excuses. 'I do not know how to speak, for I am only a youth' (1:6). Jeremiah pleaded his inexperience and lack of speaking ability. It sounded humble. But God was not impressed, for he had been preparing Jeremiah particularly for this ministry. God knew what background, gifts and experience to give Jeremiah in preparation for his call. So Jeremiah, despite his apparent humility, was in reality questioning God's work in and for him. The Lord therefore strictly commanded Jeremiah, 'Do not say, "I am only a youth"' (1:7). He then told Jeremiah simply to be obedient and do what he was told, but with the reassuring promise that 'I am with you to deliver you' (1:8).

Jeremiah 1:5

... what sort of people has God caused us to be?

A close friend of mine once shouted angrily at me, 'It's all right for you. You don't have my background.' Actually her unhappy childhood had prepared her superbly for the particular social ministry which God had given her.

In looking for God's guidance it is important to ask, 'In his sovereign control over our personal development, what has he been preparing us for?'

Use common sense

God has made us in his image. He abounds in warmth and personality, not sitting coldly on some remote Mount Olympus as an unthinking, unfeeling, Ultimate Reality. The Bible constantly affirms that God determines to do certain things. He has a mind and uses it. Created in his image, we too are called to think critically and make wise decisions.

Let us take the example of relationships. How do we know that one particular person is right for us? The Bible does give some fundamental principles. It makes it clear that we are not to 'be mismated with unbelievers', for the apostle realistically points out that such mixed marriages between a Christian and a non-Christian lack any deep unity of heart. They will lack agreement on all sorts of subjects – use of money, choice of friends, what they do on Sundays and in the evenings. Indeed they will find that they serve different masters. What a recipe for disaster!

2 Cor. 6:14 RSV

What a recipe for disaster!

But the Bible does not tell us precisely which person is to be our life partner. How then do we discover God's will in this vital matter?

Your life partner

First, we want to be confident of love. Do both partners really love each other? 1 Corinthians 13 gives us some good tests. For example, 'love is not self-seeking' – is that true of our behaviour towards each other? Love 'always protects, always trusts, always hopes' – love causes negative criticism to yield to an optimistic faith in the other person. The apostle Peter says that 'love covers over a multitude of sins' – rose-tinted glasses are a good sign of love! When Paul is talking about love in Philippians 2:3 he exhorts us to 'consider others better' than ourselves.

1 Peter 4:8

I well remember a young student coming to my study to discuss his growing attraction to a certain young woman. He said, 'I'm sure she couldn't be interested in someone like me.' It happened that the woman in question also came to see me on the very same day. She told me of her growing interest in the student who had just been talking with me. But she too doubted the possibility that he could be attracted to her, for she felt that he was far too good for her!

> ... she felt he was too good for her

Love does indeed consider the other better than ourselves. It is important that we look up to our partner as somebody we are really proud of.

While love certainly involves a very definite physical attraction and a stirring of the emotions, it also includes personal friendship.

In choosing a life partner, we face some basic questions. Do we have everyday interests in common? Can we relate to the other's social or racial background? Do we have the same basic aims in life? There are three essentials: that we love each other; that we are confident of God's leading; that we can happily anticipate a lifetime together in the everyday realities of normal life.

The New Testament makes it clear that love delights to give and to serve. The evidence and outworkings of God's love for the world was that he gave sacrificially. Jesus showed his love for us by taking the form of a servant for our sake. The media's picture of love tends to be selfish. When a man sees a pretty woman he desires her for his own self-gratification and pleasure. But as Christians we believe that love longs for the welfare and happiness of the other. We long to give pleasure to our partner and to serve them humbly for their sake. That is the mark of real love. When wondering whether we really love someone or whether they truly love us, we have here a biblical test.

John 3:16
Philippians 2:7

...the apparent foolishness of God is wiser than all our human knowledge

Conscience

In determining what course of action is right we shall not want to go against our conscience. In Romans 14:23 Paul declares that it is sin if we act with doubts of conscience and without faith.

Having said that, we need, however, to recognize that our consciences are also part of our fallen nature. They need to be educated by the constant reading and teaching of the word of God.

In this chapter, we have stressed the importance of our Gid-given minds, wisdom and common sense. And yet, the sovereign and all-powerful Lord may overrule all our carefully determined plans and so arrange our circumstances that we are pushed into apparently less sensible ways. He knows what is right in his eyes, what is best for us and for the world in which we live. Even the apparent foolishness of God is actually wiser than all our human knowledge.

1 Cor. 1:25

Many people today are sensing that purely human wisdom ultimately proves inadequate.

God is able

As Christians we are particularly aware that our common sense may not prove adequate to guide us through the maze of life's decisions. We have learned to doubt our own wisdom. Fortunately we do not need to resort to gimmicks or astrology or magic games with occult overtones. God has provided a better way. 'If any of you lacks wisdom, he should ask God, who gives generously to all without finding fault,' advises James, 'and it will be given him.' What a reassuring promise for weak mortals like ourselves! We can turn to God in humble prayer and he will give us his wisdom, so that our decisions

James 1:5

God has provided a better way

will not be made all by ourselves. They will be made *with God*. He will so work in us that his wisdom will enter into our decision-making processes. Thanks to such prayer, in line with the promise of God, we can exercise our God-given responsibility to choose, to use our common sense and what wisdom we possess.

OVER TO YOU

1. What factors in your background might be significant for your future life and work?

2. What experience and training has God arranged for you to have?

3. What gifts do you feel you have? What gifts do your friends think you have? How can these gifts be used for the glory of the Lord?

4. What are the marks and characteristics of Christian love?

Seven

Conditions for Guidance

What is the will of God for our lives? All of us face a variety of calls upon our time. What are the priorities? It is easy to allow our diaries to become overfull without serious consideration of what God really wants us to be doing. What can we do to avoid this?

Prayer – get the habit

It may prove helpful to spend a day in quiet unhurried prayer and meditation in the presence of the Lord. One after the other the various sides of our lives can be mentioned before the Lord and then in the silence we could spend as long as we want on each subject. Our minds might consider what a new meeting would mean for us – how many would we attend? How much time do they take up? Are they strategic? Do we feel at home in such meetings? Do we feel a sense of peace that this is

What are the priorities?

God's calling to us? Should we then be doing more of this sort of work? Or less? At the end of a day of such meditation on the different aspects of our life we may well feel more confident of the will of God for us.

In the New Testament fasting is not just a spiritual discipline to teach us self-control, but it is closely associated with prayer. Prayer and fasting together in unhurried fellowship with God can unravel many knotty problems. The way ahead may become clearer.

As we pray, we are expecting God to mould our thinking to fit the patterns of his will for us. As we saw earlier, the Christian mind is formed by the teaching of Scripture. Our prayer, therefore, will be based on our overall knowledge of the mind of Christ as seen in the Bible.

As we pray about our lives, it may prove helpful to consider what God has done through history. It is often said that history repeats itself. This is certainly true in the saga of church history. And yet, many today are praying about their relationship to their church without any consideration of church history. With a reasonable knowledge of the subject we may be able to pray with greater insight and so come to wiser decisions.

Do we feel a sense of peace?

Many of us have been stimulated and guided in our prayers by the example of other Christians. Biographies of significant Christians may provide direction for our prayers. How did God lead them? What was their experience of the Lord and his dealings with them? We may ask the Lord in prayer what lessons he wants us to learn from men and women whose life-stories have been written up for us.

> ...it is the meek and humble who will inherit the earth

Humility first

We should not think that God will only guide us if we fulfil certain preconditions. And yet it is also true that the Bible teaches some principles which may facilitate God's guiding word being heard.

King David points out in Psalm 25:9 that God 'guides the humble in what is right, and teaches them his way'.

As we acknowledge our weakness and need of the Lord's loving guidance, we shall be more likely to hear his word to us. The same Hebrew word for 'humble' is also used in Psalms 76:9 and 149:4 which declare that God gives his salvation to the meek. Amazingly too it is the meek and humble who will inherit the earth. Humility is a basic precondition for salvation, guidance and a ministry of influence in the world.

Obedience and forgiveness

Psalm 25:9 leads on in the following verse to the affirmation that the Lord's 'ways' are full of love and faithfulness for those 'who keep the demands of his covenant'. We cannot expect the

Lord graciously to guide us unless we are willing to be obedient. Such obedience will surely issue out from a genuine love for the Lord mingled with a deep sense of awe. Proverbs 1:7 points out that 'the fear of the Lord is the beginning of knowledge'. Such humble obedience may be seen as a middle path between self-will on the one side and a masochistic desire for sacrifice on the other.

... mingled with a deep sense of awe

'I want' is not a good beginning to a prayer for guidance! 'Lord, show me your will for my life. I'll do anything for you as long as it is not . . .' No, we come before the Lord with our lives open before him.

The aim of our life is to glorify the Lord. As 1 Cor. 6:19–20 Paul says, 'you are not your own; you were bought with a price. So glorify God in your body.'

Many of us have a fear that this means God is likely to call us to do what we most dislike. If there is one thing we really don't want to do, that must surely be the Lord's will for us! As we have seen, our heavenly Father is not like that. He loves us very dearly and delights to lavish good gifts upon us. He is not an ogre who revels in torturing his people.

So the Christian should be open to the Lord for whatever he desires. All of us need constantly to say to the Lord, 'I will do anything for you and I will go anywhere you want.'

Sometimes the Lord will surprise us, so we need to be flexible in approach. Jonah was a good Jew and it never occurred to him that God might send him to preach to Gentiles, but he did. If we are too rigid in what we expect from the Lord, we too may get a shock or two! Be ready for anything in the service of the Lord!

'I want' is not a good beginning

Perhaps the greatest hindrance to guidance is sin. When we are consciously living in disobedience to the revealed standards of God, we cannot expect his voice to lead us clearly. Sin blocks the ears.

When prayer is easy, then guidance also grows clearer.

Be practical

Some of us were brought up on the old slogan 'Ora et labore', 'pray and work'. It is often true that prayer should lead to active practical outworkings. In seeking God's guidance too, our humble prayers may well need to be linked to some practical steps.

When my wife and I returned to Britain after two terms of missionary service, we were very unsure of what would be our next step. Various openings were offered to us, but nothing seemed right. The months slipped by with all the heartache of uncertainty. It was at this stage

...a fear that God is likely to call us to do what we most dislike

that an older friend and Christian leader wrote to us, saying, 'God cannot steer a stationary ship. You need to go ahead and do something positive.'

It is often good to take definite steps to discover more information about the way we could take. When wondering about a job, find out more about training courses, job opportunities and what life would really be like. It may be right to actually apply for particular posts and see what doors open.

Patience, advice and pieces of paper

As Christians, we believe that God has a spec-ific path prepared for us. It is unseemly therefore to engage in a feverish search for an open door.

Isaiah 64:4 God 'works for those who wait for him'. Sometimes it's right to stand back from a frenetic search for God's will and wait patiently and prayerfully for the Lord to act on our behalf.

We are called to be fellow-workers with Christ, and not just passive objects.

It is hard to know how to pray when we face difficult decisions, particularly when our emotions are deeply involved in the decision. We may find it helpful to write down on paper what possible paths could lie ahead, or make a list of the advantages and disadvantages for each possible choice. This may facilitate intelligent prayer as we seek the will of the Lord.

... a frenetic search for God's will ...

How to be a living sacrifice

We have already observed how Paul firmly believed that God's will is 'good, pleasing and perfect'. *Romans 12:2*

There is a neat symmetry in the first two verses of Romans 12:

> 'Therefore, I urge you, brothers, in view of God's mercy, to offer your bodies as living sacrifices, holy and pleasing to God – this is your spiritual act of worship. Do not conform any longer to the pattern of this world, but be transformed by the renewing of your mind. Then you will be able to test and approve what God's will is – his good, pleasing and perfect will.'

Because A is true, therefore do B; do C and thus experience D. A and D are closely related, as are also B and C. In diagrammatic form:

A in view of God's mercy,   *therefore do –*
B offer your bodies as living
   sacrifices,   *do –*
C be transformed by the
   renewing of your mind.   *and thus*
D what God's will is.   *experience*

Paul appeals to us to present our bodies 'as living sacrifices'. As with sacrifices dedicated to the Lord in the temple, so our bodies are to be holy. In the service of Christ there can be no easygoing tolerance of sin. When presented to the Lord, our bodies belong utterly to him. Our own desires or preferences count for nothing. We belong entirely to him. So in looking for God's guidance we need constantly to remember that our bodies have been tied to the sacrificial altar as an offering for him for his service. We can no longer look selfishly for our own self-fulfilment, comfort or career prospects, but we humbly ask, 'Lord, what do you want me to do? And where do you want me to serve you? Anything, anywhere.' This, Paul says, is our 'spiritual worship'. We hear much these days about worship and its importance in the church. Romans 12:1 teaches us what is the fundamental nature of truly spiritual worship.

Do not conform any longer ...

The offering of our bodies is here closely associated with a right use of our minds. How we think determines what we do. We cannot separate the sacrifice of our bodies from a renewed mind which will transform our whole life. No longer are we to be 'conformed to this world'. In an age when we are bombarded by the media, advertisements and fashion-consciousness it is not easy to discern how far the world is influencing our thought patterns and therefore our attitudes and behaviour. But Paul exhorts us constantly to exercise biblical Christian thinking in all things.

... bombarded by the media ...

We are being asked to abandon not only sinful habits of thought and action – they may be fairly easy to recognize if not to give up – but also attitudes which in themselves may seem harmless. It may never have occurred to us to question them. They are an ordinary fact of everyday living.

Now that we have seen a little more of what it means to prove or experience what God's will is, we must return to the main question of this book: How do we discover God's guidance? Perhaps the key to this question lies in Romans 12:1–2. We need first to soak ourselves in the biblical teaching concerning God's universal purposes of mercy, his will for the world and for his church. Only then should we be praying about our own part in the development of the whole history of God's relationship to his people. We will then ask the Lord how we personally fit into his overall purposes. What does he want to do for the world and the church, or for our own family, local situation or

God himself will surely direct us

congregation? In this broader context the apostle Paul appeals to us to present our bodies as living sacrifices – and God himself will then surely direct us and instruct us according to his will.

Further Reading

G. Friesen, *Decision Making and the Will of God* (Multnomah Press, 1980).

E.V. Goldsmith, *God Can Be Trusted* (OM Publishing, 1974, 2003).

M.C. Griffiths, *Don't Soft-pedal God's Call* (OMF, 1968).

M.C. Griffiths, *Give Up Your Small Ambitions* (IVP, 1970).

M.C. Griffiths, *Take My Life* (IVP/STL, 1967).

OMF, *When God Guides* (OMF, 1984).

T. Partridge, *Choosing Your Vocation* (Marshalls, 1982).

M. Blaine Smith, *Knowing God's Will* (Ark Publishing, 1980).

G. Christian Weiss, *The Perfect Will of God* (Moody Press, 1950).

D. Willard, *In Search of Guidance* (Regal Books, 1984).

Books by Martin and Elizabeth Goldsmith

Against All Odds (Authentic Media/OMF, 2007).

Get a Grip on Mission (IVP/OMF, 2006).

God Can Be Trusted (OM Publishing, 1974, 2003).

Good News for All Nations (Hodder, 2002).

Islam and Christian Witness (OM Publishing, 1974, 2003).

Jesus and His Relationships (Paternoster, 2000).

Life's Tapestry (Authentic Media, 1997, 2006).

Matthew and Mission (Paternoster, 2001).

Roots and Wings (OM Publishing, 1998).

What About Other Faiths? (Hodder, 1989, 2003).

Who Is My Neighbour? (Authentic Media, 1988, 2007).